Bowing to

June Hall lives in Bath with her novelist husband, Greg, and when they're around, her son, Richard (20) and daughter, Katherine (18). She began her career in the editorial department at Faber & Faber where she eventually became an editor before moving into paperback publishing and eventually setting up a literary agency which was later to merge with the giant, PFD in 1988.

Major life events have inevitably shaped her subject matter – in particular the stillbirth of her first son, Philip, and her own diagnosis of Parkinson's Disease in 1996 – both led to writing poetry again and publishing in various magazines. This is her second collection, following *The Now of Snow* in 2004.

Also by June Hall: *The Now of Snow*

Praise for *The Now of Snow*:

'The book's title suggests transience, while the poem of that title fixes the importance of a single, shining moment. The line of footprints on the cover says it without any words at all, each one a little Now that is part of an individual progression.

The first poems in the book are single steps into the reality of Parkinson's Disease: diagnosis, curiosity, self-pity, defiance and the huge responsibility of telling beloved others, a step at a time.

There are poems of family, of the tragedy of loss and the unfolding miracle of change; poems that slot into the white spaces between rites of passage. Later, the poet looks at art with unapologetic subjectivity and at world-shattering atrocity with a calm appraisal that mixes horror and truth. And truth is the cornerstone of the volume.

Each poem, true to the book's epigraph from the teachings of Zen master Thich Nhat Hanh, embraces a present moment but together they show us that, inevitably, Now is a moveable feast.'
ANN DRYSDALE.

'June Hall's poetry evokes memories and emotions which move the reader. She startles and satisfies with unexpected phrases.'
PATRICIA OXLEY, *Acumen*

'I do like her work – it has tremendous punch and manages to be both humorous and tragic simultaneously.'
WANDA BARFORD

and support for *Bowing to Winter*:

'Everyone at the Parkinson's Disease Society is delighted that June's moving poems will again support essential research. This book will be a great success.'
RICHARD BRIERS

Bowing
to
Winter

JUNE HALL

BELGRAVE
PRESS·BATH

BELGRAVE PRESS • BATH   7 BELGRAVE ROAD, BATH BA1 6LU
in association with Melia Publishing

Copyright © June Hall 2010

First published 2010 by
Belgrave Press, Bath
7 Belgrave Road,
Bath,
BA1 6LU

in association with Melia Publishing Services

(both not now accepting submissions)

A catalogue record for this book is available from the British
Library

ISBN 978-0-9546215-1-3
EAN   9780954621513

Cover design and typesetting by
Paul Mitchell Design Ltd. 01628 664011

Printed in Great Britain by
Cromwell Press Group, Trowbridge, Wilts.

In memory of

UA

most generous of tutors and mentors
to whom I'm lovingly indebted
for her teaching,
support
and
inspiration

Acknowledgements

Thanks to the editors of the following magazines in which some of these poems have appeared: *Acumen, Agenda, Artemis, Equinox, Envoi, French Literary Review, Orbis, Poetry Scotland, De Facto, Interpreter's House, Coffee House Poetry, Bath Dharma Journal*

Spree Fever won the Torbay Poetry Challenge in 2005 and *First Meeting* was one of the three runners-up in the Mervyn Peake 2009 poetry competition; *A Lipping Moon* was long-listed for the Virginia Warbey in 2006 and won joint 1st place in the *Orbis* Readers' Award 2009; *Cow-Time* appeared in the anthology, *Only Connect* (ed Ashton & Fortune-Wood, Cinnamon Press, 2007) and *Real Estate Tango* in the anthology, *Cracking On* (ed Joy Howard, Grey Hen Press, 2009)

Heartfelt thanks to Maggie Butt, Penelope Shuttle, Tim Liardet and Greta Stoddart who all helped to make this collection better than it would otherwise have been; to all at the Bath Poetry Café, Poetry Surgery and Poetry Cam; warm appreciation to the following friends, colleagues and teachers for their support, encouragement and challenges: Rosie Bailey, Ann Drysdale, Berna Fitzgerald, Julia Green, Christine Jump, Frances-Anne King, Patricia and William Oxley, Felicity Perera; of course to my family, Greg, Richard and Katherine Hall (severe but perceptive critics); and last but not least, to Paul Mitchell for his cover design, and Terry Melia, Billy Adair and other members of Melia Publishing Services for their enthusiasm and professionalism.

Contents

From the withered tree
a flower blooms.

Shoyoroku

I

Bath-Time

Gran was bulk, padding, rough tweed
to my mother's pink silk and ballerina froth.

She was a church-going woman, duty

stitched into her hems, polished into post-war
brogues and darned with large sampler stitches
into navy cardigan and thick beige stockings.

Hers weren't the arms I wanted as I wept
(Mum already half way to London to try her luck
at the single life), but she rubbed kind words

into me with a loofah, soaped me with rhymes,
planted me on the wide acreage of her lap;
wedged between broad-bank thighs. I let her

bury me in layers of rough white bath towel
like a milk-tooth folded deep in a grown-up hanky,
hiding its tiny, blood-stained stump.

Shivers

Stun of current in green-streaming Wye.
Not plunging, foot-faulting. Pigeon toes slip on weed,
tipping pock-marked rocks under rolling arches.

*

Victorian basement hung with damp. Skinny Liz, me,
slow to strip, swallowed by claw-foot bath, its metal
unwarmed by jugs of water choked from tetchy geezer.

*

Crunch of beach in summer sandwiches. Fish paste smells
blown away on wind-bitten sand. Crone-child, draped
in towels heavy with wet, smitten with shivering fever.

*

Mother, returning. Panic I've slid off the pier like
a coffin, unwatched. Wrong road taken. Finding each
other in gale-force winds, her arms hug in my shivers.

*

Small shakes play grandmother's footsteps, creep up on
the decades. Full-grown, they co-habit - skin-twitching,
hand-rolling, foot-jerking - restless squatters who won't go.

Seeds

From interlacing grasses tall as we were we picked
    woody stalks for fencing foils, ran finger
and thumb down long, brittle stems,
      stripping off hairy seeds, hiding clusters
in catapult-tense fists, loaded for sudden ambush.

We sneezed, exploding seed-bombs that scattered
and landed in laughing mouths, dived free-falling
      inside open-necked shirts, wriggled under
vests, down pants, tickling young flesh to
    a crescendo of snorts and squeals. At two pm

the Convent bell tolled to halt such wildness.

    Sister Angela, armoured in starched white wimple
and layers of black serge, rounded up for catechism
      her possible future brides of Christ – in fact
C of E kids confettied with grass seeds.

First Ball

You make my juices flow, boy, rush like river rapids,
you, surfing the New Year Ball, riding my dreams,
with danger-red sash, hair sleek with gloss, and tomcat eyes

flashing animal signs to dissolve me. Tight-partnered,
we twist and dive; you lift and dip me - your first, your best,
your white-water wonder-girl. In the melt of a waltz you float

me off the floor, swing me through flash-flooding reels till,
squeezed dizzy with body heat and whirlpools of longing,
I sink down deep, know I'd let go, drown for you...

...but − new year still virginal - quick and cool as a snow-cat,
you shake yourself dry and are gone. Ice seals my letterbox:
the phone I shiver over frozen

A Lipping Moon

His clisp was pure honey; she was chiffed to the core,
they twichered till sunset and still wanted more
and with the moon lipping in wide purple sky
they grauped and snugdoodled – no need to ask why.

As the barnable clunked and they heard the chimes crink
he pressfully asked: *shall we wed, do you think?*
With crumping arm round her, his chapper alert,
they tangoed and tangled and squiffed till it hurt.

His cheek chuffed with hers, their feet slithered and flicked
and the orchestra's drums would rumbum as they kicked
Then she said that she would – or would if he would.
When the hazy plink yawned – both knew that they should.

And so they were married, coombe-fingled by boat
to the Isles in the West on which seals gload the moat
round a castle sea-white on moon-lipping shores
where they tangoed and slupped to night's wild-water roars.

My Real Skinny Self

A wisp of a girl who's grown a tad stout,
once I was scrawny, limbs bare as a pin,
now my real skinny self yearns to get out.

I'll eat only greens, eat less, go without,
but die for choc'late – such cardinal sin –
I'm a wisp of a girl grown a tad stout.

Once geisha-gorgeous, I'd party and pout,
flaunt silky ball-gowns – chassé and spin:
that slinky-young-self still yearns to get out.

Press-ups and pull-ins aren't routines to flout;
I'll work on love handles, wobbling chin,
a must for a wisp who's grown a tad stout;

I'll go to the gym, de-tox and work out –
until I lose tons, all cakes I shall bin
'cos my twiggy-young-self's mad to get out.

I'm a blubbery whale starting to spout
in a sea full of minnows dashingly thin,
I'm a wisp of a girl grown a tad stout:
will my real skinny self ever get out?

School Centenary

Old girls, tipped into midlife – or worse – by wine,
divorce or just the flurry of years, we dip and dive,
heave and elbow, rummaging round the school hall
through the years set out on trestle tables –
lost bits and pieces of childhood to reclaim.

A patchwork of cuttings on cork news-boards pins down
a century in monochrome – decades of girls in rows,
once monitored for squeaks, giggles, chats and dares,
now sit in sepia silence. I smile, being my own
research project, and pounce on a class snap

which walks me backwards till I bump into a younger self,
leggy child, limbs knotted, toes tucked up on her chair,
twiggy hand doodling on a jotter. History suddenly links
not just back but on through the chain of dna
to an undreamt future presaged in the photo by the way

my long-boned son twists and uncurls our wiry body while
his hand shields eyes with which we squint as one into the sun.

Moments

M oments when no-one else will do
O therwise I shrink to age six – a year waiting,
T wisted in tears under scullery slabs.
H ow will it be when you die on me?
E very Christmas there you are in your chair,
R eading *The Telegraph*, mending my skirts.

Father

You were my mother's hate man.
I grew to hate you too.
You were a blank, a space,
the only sound from you:
money talk, clinking coins,
the silent cheque that never came.

Here is an SOS

Will his daughter, last seen as a baby
in South Africa fifty years ago,
please go at once to Sydney, Australia,
where her father is dangerously old.

Demobbed

Striped,
brass-buttoned and bonded in vanity,
they wangled foreign postings
and danced the war away
in a land of plenty.

Afterwards
in the rubble of the late forties
when everything was dusty and tired
and fun strictly rationed, they sailed again
for the Cape of Good Hope

unprepared
for the humdrum of marriage;
stripped to civvy greys,
tilting at teaching and prep,
they stumbled on unfamiliar steps

till, quick of heel,
he spun from milk-dribbling breasts
to new manoeuvres, fresh arms – and eyes
in whose bright mirror he saw himself –
still in full plumage.

The Man-Woman Puzzle

Men eat more and fart easily in company,
Women watch their figures
and eat water-biscuits without butter.

Men bulge over armrests in tubes or theatres,
their elbows jab the adjoining spaces
while women pull in their arms,
hardly breathe, shrink into themselves.

Men like to limber up in the morning,
argue with the radio or do press-ups.
Women struggle to consciousness
and poke the children out of bed.

Women like to speak to other women,
warm, heart-sharing stuff, but hold back
if men are about, let them go first.

Men like women to like them
and vice versa – no argument there.

Men get to the newspaper first but keep
the pages orderly. Women only reach it
late at night but then they mess it up
or use it to wipe the cat's sick.

Men are muscley, heady, crappy.
Like exotic plants women look good
but die without nourishment.

Women may be fleshy or skinny,
dressy or depressed. As they stir the porridge
they dream or hide their anger.

Men know strings of jokes, hide their isms
behind laughter. Women freeze when
asked to be funny, forget the punchlines.

Men make the world go round
and so do women.

Men and women fit together
like two halves of a Chinese puzzle –
and sometimes they don't.

First Meeting

A kiss petals my cheek in unexpected greeting.
Under the sun's rising fire your smile grows looser,
arresting as Chinese lanterns that release their mauves,
water-pinks and rain-streaked purples into the land.

In the tropical hothouse of the season our first encounter
is tentative – though eager – like that of rainforest birds,
and just as spring surprises, blossoming into cherry, so you
burst into fun and your special gift of full-blown laughter.

His Underpants

hang pegged on the line while we play tennis,
snoozing like baby hedgehogs, pale blue,
a nursery snuggled close in the sun,
held in the fine mesh of a laundry bag.

You think you'll get them dry in there? I lob
(off-court). *Dunno – that's women's work!*
Will the wife scoop them up then, cramped
from their lunchtime nap or settle these warm

though damp balls to burrow down again?
They're not yours, of course? Chip and chase.
He simply blocks, grinning at me,
saving his fancy footwork for another game.

I dream the sleepers uncurl by night, snuffle off.
Without them he concedes – game, set and match,
washes his own underpants, pegs them out to dry,
loud and laddish as flag-waving fans, Centre Court.

II

Empty

Where does the spiral begin or end –
      with the twist of a conch,
with a foetal curl?

      You lived and died
womb-bound
      as the November tides turned.
Here on an empty kitchen floor
      two black tails trace question-marks,
cats punctuate our grief,
      their cries high-pitched like babies'.

The new cot's gone,
      a blue blanket all that's left
and a post-mortem result that claims:
      non-viable and *no answers* –
a pronouncement that
      juts and scrapes,
hollow as bare bones, stripped by sea.

      My still-rounded body
from which your tiny form was cut
      is a spiral of *whys,*
a shock of echoes.

Bowing to Winter

White infant-coffin with grown-up silver name-plate;
breasts that leaked and dribbled, unsucked;
a need crying in every nerve – yet for all this,

nothing could make your heart beat again or put the leaves
back on the November branches or, with the turn of the month,
make the hanging of Christmas holly bearable.

Like sweets in wartime, though, I hoarded
scores of unexpected letters, rationing myself to one a day.
I never knew I had so many weeks of friendship –

I bow to them now: to the surgeon who cried delivering you;
the nurses who took your picture and lifted you into
your father's arms, he, stooping to gather you;

bow to an ending that preceded a beginning;
to the cold time of not-knowing, the barren place of waiting,
bow to winter – and to rare flashes of spring.

An Alphabet for You

i.m. Philip Hall, stillborn Nov 1987

A is for Arms that sag, yearning for weight;
B is for a Birth – though not Breathing or Breath;
C marks your Cot with Candle-lit vigil;
D is for Death – how it's Darkened your skin.

E is for Earth where your ashes will bloom;
F is for Friends whose letters flower daily;
G is for Gossamer, limbs that may snap;
H is for Heart – no sound of life lapping.

I is for Illness and Illness Ignored;
J is all Jelly – the shaking won't stop;
K's for the Kisses we feather you with;
L is for Love that's fountaining through me.

M is for Milk – breasts that weep for your lips;
N's for November that binds birth with death;
O is for Oughts – guilt-shaped by so many;
P's for your name, Pip, clipped like your life.

Q is for Quickening, kicks never felt;
R is for Rage, Red poppies, Remembrance;
S for the Surgeon who says he might cry;
T for Transparent – skin that may crumble.

U's for Unfair and Unfair and Unfair;
V's a Virus that kills you – but not me;
W - Womb – a conch full of echoes;
X ticks a box that calls you non-viable;

Y is for Yelps and a howl in the gut;
Z is for
            Zero,
                    Zilch

27

A Death, A Birth

Unstoppable,
shivers drummed through me
when my first son was cut,
dead,
from my body.

My heart burnt
all through that leafless, winter season.

This summer
the surgeon sliced into my womb again
and a fanfare of blood sprayed
over the green cloth wall on my stomach;

this time,
like a celebrant at the high altar,
he held you up to your father,
gowned in green,
who wept and beamed

as he planted you,
a slip of a stranger,
to slither and mewl on my chest.

Sensing the tug
between fragile tissue
and survival,
I trembled for this battle
(lost in stillbirth
by your brother),

yet now love riots:
shoots of new-life spring up
and I open to
a white wilderness flowering.

III

Ice Cream in the Rain

Now, they urge. *Why not?*
Anoraks shine, streaming blue.
Smiles lick wet faces.

Down-Under

The Royal Couple's First Train Tour:
a tribute to Her Majesty on her 80th birthday

Strap-hanging, in love,
they spy a flag of live sheep
dyed blue, white and red.

White-gloved, the young queen waves, her
smile rippling round the Empire.

Copycat

Her snow-pick eyes dig deep, fixed on mine.
I've got a shake too! she quivers,
unclasping our limb-lock, rolling on her back
curly with giggles. She maps the sky:

Look – there's God!

           Hoots at a cloud full of sun,

easy with the shifting landscape of our lives
so long as love holds steady to its pulse.
I squeeze her youngness, kiss her warmth –
my turn to mould myself to her bloom.

Letting Go of God

I don't want to bother God. She shrugs away
the busy bureaucrat with big-bang temper
glimpsed through her disbelief.

Can he have slipped away,
a laugh tickling his lips,
leaving us only the language of silence?

A Certain Slant

(with apologies to Emily Dickinson)

There's a certain Slant of light,
Sunday Afternoons –
That exposes pock-marked Paint,
Spots like wizened Prunes.

Sagging paper, ripe with Mould –
Damp brings up Despair –
Means we cannot fix the Rot
Breathing in the Stair.

The Spirit-level shows how
Sick Wood's out of true –
Each Blow sent to test us – till –
We Restore – Renew.

Spree Fever

For Katherine on her first visit to New York

You must go down to the shops again,
           to the heaving crowds and the queues
and all you seek are the chic boutiques
           and designer labels to choose
with bargains galore – since the dollar's weak –
           and your blue eyes set on spending
and the call of the diner – with all you can eat –
           and a subway ride still pending.

You must go down to the shops again,
           to Tiffany's, Macy's and Saks
for the silk culottes and chiffon gowns
           and the satin sandals in racks
and all you want are Armani jeans,
           worn-washed with mirror-beads gloating
and a red halter-top and a crystal watch
           and clouds of perfume floating.

You must go down to the fashion halls –
           Galliano, Chanel and Dior –
to try Gucci boots and cashmere suits
           and crushed velvet capes you'll adore
and all you ask is for peer-group gasps
           as you give out your Bloomingdale bags,
and for feet – a rest, a vote for 'best-dressed'
           and the dream of *couturier* tags.

Nobody Listens

She will nag but she never listens.
It's all: *pick your things up; tidy your room;
do this, do that.* So annoying!
says I'm a slob but she's the mother –
I'm not a housewife, it's not my job.
I'm *me*, fifteen soon – not some little kid.

My own good? Who's she trying to kid –
ranting and raving? Who listens
to me? They can fight but we can't. Good job
I can plug in and get away to my room.
I would have to have a geriatric mother
with no idea how annoying

she is - like my piggy sister – just as annoying –
squealing and telling tales – *the darling kid.*
I want to push her fat face in, tell my Mother
what she's really like but Mum's not one who listens
even when she comes for a *chat* in my room.
Well, why should I look after Fatty? It's not my job!

Dad's no help – you'd think it might be his job!
Just had a holiday but he still finds us all annoying.
He's not ill now but he's always in his room –
online – till she drags him out. So, who's the kid?
Does what he's told – when he listens,
Why not stand up to her? She's not his mother.

She would have to be sick. Who needs a mother
who goes and talks on all that stuff – as a job –
on the radio while the whole world listens?
So not-cool. And she says I'm annoying –
goes on and on at me – like I'm a stupid kid;
preaches *respect* then barges into my room –

no knock. Too mean, of course, to decorate this room.
Do it on a budget! she says – <u>so</u> like my mother!
I'd have to use my own money same as my kid-
sister, who may be dumb – but painting's not my job
No way. Plain bloody annoying
always getting on to me – but nobody listens.

OK, I'll tidy my room - I don't care! I've got a job –
six quid an hour, dear mother! Not so annoying
now, am I? – not just a kid. Now let's see who listens!

Boy

grown tall on trouble,
you head on up,
wind-scorched and starved of sky
but I remember
twiggy branches stretching
out their curious buds
and – floating towards me –
the shy scent of a sapling
once brilliant with bees and light.

Little Man

Little man, what changed you?
Do you know what changed you?
Gave you lips to pull a sneer,
Picking quarrels, swilling beer;
Gave you hands to roll a spliff,
Made you hot-tongued in a tiff.
Once you were my bright-eyed child,
Cautious, if not meek and mild.
Little man, what changed you?
Do you know what changed you?

Little man, I'll tell you,
Little man, I'll tell you:
Hormones sluice you day and night,
Testosterone will cause a fight.
High on grass and blind to danger,
Weaving dreams, my six-foot stranger:
You a child and I your mother,
Butting heads, we hurt each other.
Little man, God help us.
Little man, God help us.

Remnants

Slashing through neon, the neat blade glides,
easy-slitting and quick as a tailor at his cloth.
A sharp ear might have caught the swish of air
in the flash before the fine edge slips, slicing flesh
to open the underlying brightness of the boy
that bubbles, wet and brotherly as beer-foam.

Stained in a moment when friendship tripped
and fractured, the steel knife spins to the gutter
while cries dwindle, dropping to a wheeze, a whisper,
and urgency, hinted in the eyes, clouds over.
Stunned girls scarper, skirts kicking up round thighs;
bottles tipped at lips, alcohol burning in

red-lit eyes, shooting the bright-flow rapids
of the veins. A sweet repellent smell of vomit
leans into the wind and the wail of police sirens
picks up and amplifies the dazed breathing of the street
and odd moans of two youths now mere bags
of bone – and rags trimmed to blood-soaked remnants.

Blood Rain

Rain brightens and batters late peonies, crimson
as blood cupped in soft-petal bowls; bold

as freshly glossed lips. I hear, or half-hear, news
of Israel's birthday: sixty years of children dying

in crossfire; sixty years since hope was born
to a country, somehow, always in mourning.

Petals scatter, whipped by the storm. Some spike
on barbed-wire fencing; stalks snap like dandelions

plucked and discarded by youngsters on picnics.
Rain won't stop – which leads to flash-flooding.

IV

Hotel on the Square

Antibes 2007

Provence. Barely dawn. A platform suspended
outside my bedroom window. Tree surgeons
in blue overalls. Vibrations from grinding chainsaws.
Stalls not yet set up below with the usual clack

and clatter. Strange time to pollard the lime trees
that hem and shape the square, cutting into the sleepiness
of holiday makers before they can breathe the mix
of morning smells: citrus fruits, sharp coffee,

acrid cigarette smoke. The high-pitched whine drills
into my dreamscape, bores into old terrors. Still half
asleep, I'm child again having teeth pulled under gas
as amputations crash past: fingers of sawn-off branches,

knuckles and elbows, smash on the terrace below.
At my window a nightmare threat of the dental chair
recreates from early Convent days – falling into Hell.
But before August can boil over, we find a new hotel.

Mistral

Forest pine shivers
frisked by rough summer winds;
elbows soon bend.

Out of Season

A drift of pigeons
slides from hot pantiled roof –
melt of summer snow.

Alone

Outside mistral flaps,
scorpions scuttle;
we two sit silent.

Epiphany

Let them go: the shopping, tills and trolleys,
collection points and credit cards, gift wrap, present lists –
a craziness called Christmas.

Open instead to a topsy-turvy landscape where
midday spring somersaults over winter into a world
of lavender, freshly planted, near winter pansies;
of birdsong and raucous cicadas, blanched limestone,
almond orchards dreaming blossom sleep; an olive grove
that bides its time and the bright lane with red-earth trail
left by the post-girl's scooter as it bumps and chokes
through leafless vines fringed by catkins.

The house phone begins to nag. To mark Epiphany
the children will munch *galettes des Rois* tonight
and search the dough for *santons*; I'll take our cards down
though in the village some Christmas lights will linger,
their colours stretching from one season to the next.

Critical voices chant mantras in my head as the phone insists
but it's the sun at my back that gently pushes me indoors.
So Epiphany brings its own revelation –
not the time-out I expected – yet whether
creatively adrift or floating in Nature's unexpected hold,
I am learning nothing – and – everything.

Two Seasons

Hot leather –
sandals make
a weave of light.
Summer's burning skin,
well oiled, breaths
wild air spiced by thyme
and lavender.

Winter's season
smells of log smoke,
skulking,
fur in dark wardrobes,
vests and ear muffs,
sulking time.

They never meet.

Left

flopped like beanbags
for two childless days of sun,
we know flesh will burn.

Summer Solstice

Summer breaks in half.
Sun irons cloth of picnic gold;
folds it away burnt.

July

Land in hot coma
waits. Cicadas saw the thick air,
restless for waking.

Real Estate Tango

South of France

Remembering whistled cat-calls of warm-skinned Latins, lightly,
as into waltz-time or a slow foxtrot, I glide into flirtation,
an art to be savoured like that forgotten aphrodisiac, temptation.

I'm not daft – it's my euros not my baggy body he's after,
this turn-me-on, wink-to-win, forty-plus agent – but in the South,
dressed, undressed by sun, years ripen women to autumnal

perfection. Tipsy on giggles, intent on buying *a proper view*,
I whirl about, measuring views. We heel-turn and feather-step
on a medley of balconies while he displays his best apartments,

whisks tango in my blood, footwork super-smooth as he leads
in a swirl of link, stalk and pivot steps to the wild tempo
of a finale in which he swivels, spins, catches me – a done deal.

Adieu

We pack August away with the swim things, piles
of suitcases, beach balls, French phrase books.
The barbecue is banished to the barn, pool chairs
stacked, lilos deflated, wasps swatted and squashed.
The car overflows with a wave of outdoor toys
crested by a pair of small jelly shoes, florescent lime
with sand still sticking to them – a reminder
of pocket money rows, laughter and moon-paddling.

Children eating plums dash in and out the house as rain
hops and bounces off fig leaves, shining them up, wiping
the season clean. Swallows start to cross the Sahara
and wet gives way to the kick of a flash wind from Africa,
coating us in red dust while it flaps and tugs at loose rope
on the roof-rack as we leave the barefoot life, drive into
pale English light, heading north for home and forgotten
rhythms of alarm clocks, school runs, grey winter uniforms.

V

Mrs Dribbles

Mrs Dribbles was shuffling downstairs one morning,
unaware of the salty beard forming around her chin.
The saliva filling her mouth blurred her speech slightly
when the phone rang to tell her she should have been –

elsewhere. Mrs Muddles stared in dismay at her diary.
The original appointment was clearly written in;
the changed date, which she'd now missed, wasn't.
How on earth could she have been such a fool again?

Dear Mrs Under-drugged, said her Consultant, *The time
has come to celebrate the wonders of science. Believe me,
this new drug, though much maligned by the press, is
a good drug. You cannot buy Time by not taking it.*

Former Mrs Businesswoman and Entrepreneur, now
Mrs PD, knew when she was beat. The time had come.
Give me the pills, she said, hobbling over to look at
the tiny blue-grey capsules, and went home with them, shaking.

Night

wipes the mind clean, brushes through sleep,
mopping into cobwebbed corners;
dusts off dreams and clears the vacant hours,
drums upon the morning.

Morning

Harbour village wakes
to bracken light and mist;
kippers smoke.

October Cobweb

Rain sparkling on lace;
beaded walkways on which to dance,
deadly in beauty.

Ten Years On

You're looking fine – you seem the same.
Oh come on, please! Give me a break!
The cure's so close, the papers claim.

PD? Of course it's hard to name.
Why whisper? Is it for my sake?
You're looking fine – you seem the same.

It's true you're in a waiting game.
I look blank-faced and un-awake....
The cure's so close, the papers claim.

We all lose track – age is to blame.
I can't disguise mistakes I make.
You're looking fine – you seem the same

New stem-cell labs get world acclaim.
But news of break-through is a fake.
The cure's so close, the papers claim.

The new drugs...? No? Well, that's a shame.

It's hard to know which pills to take.
I don't look fine; don't feel the same.
The cure's not close – don't play that game!

51

Un-noticed

how two saliva streams slip and drip their way to meet
like the messy mouth-melt of a child's ice cream,
and how I flick away wet ends that run beneath my chin;

or how a hanging cave mouth gapes; or smile droops,
slipped loose as a toddler's wayward lace, waiting to trip
– if not hitched and tied – with casual double-knotting.

Sometimes in the mirror, eyes blank back at me until,
mustering all muscle-slack, I learn to fake a new mouth,
paint a grinning arc on up-curled lips while shadows

hover round the mask, which, when it drops,
exposes the sag and drag of an unknown face. But nobody
notices my stare – or how the wind has changed.

Wheelchair Wars

for all in wheelchairs

Bickering burns the air. Sparks from
a clash of tongues light up the bystanders,
who, though singed, pretend indifference.
Would we be addicted to point-scoring
like this couple if I were in a wheelchair,
my feet and legs, bloated like hers,
were sausaged into joggers and slipper socks
like a guy stuffed for burning?

Or what if my husband and bicker-partner,
a smile smeared indelibly on his face,
were chained to my penned-in, pent-up body,
as he hitched and tipped the wheelchair,
dodging my snarls, his tired eyes hidden,
face averted in a spiral of frustration?

Would he, companion, soul-mate, be trapped
into snap-and-score carer? Would I begin to hiss
orders in the silence seething between us
or crack out my fury in finger-bone clicks?
Would we train in squabbling to Olympic standards:
fire volleys of high-scoring sighs, keep a tally
of reproach? How would we score our joint captivity?

Chronic

Sure, I've tried not to gulp down the dark sticky facts
spooned out by doctors – fear flaring like an angry rash –

tried to deny the chronic disease label, yet just as a medicine's
after-taste may kick in, more foul than at first, so they worsen,

the symptoms: tripping on paving that flips up, smashing pain
in my face; or a comic stumble and tumble in the hedge;

waking – in the early morning in the strong arms of a tremor;
the salty glaze of a snail-trail dribbling down worn chin-paths;

voice – sounds fine to me but to others drops low with slur,
an online blur. I know because I have to repeat myself

often enough to make me fizzy as a wasp in a jam-jar,
buzzing as it throws itself unheard about its glass prison;

bladder – pushed to overflow when a stranger called Me presses
the panic button like a kid standing helpless at her own door

and a warm wetness runs away from her, filling her shoes
as she thanks God, this time, no-one's around to hear her squelch.

VI

Yellow Bird

after 'Yellow Bird', a pastel by Hugo Colville

Out of a hole in the man's chest pops a bird.
In the sag of his torso there's a hollow round the place
where smart surgeons have jig-sawed and cut away
so the tin man goes on ageing when rage bends him
squared in on himself, shoulder and elbow bent.
His cornered body, once upright and steel-strong,
now light with emptiness, is grown grey, suit-coloured,
its geometric planes drawn in pain.

Hunched, one-legged in his own shadow, he cranes
to the bird's bright wink, chin pegged to his shoulder,
a thin cushion for the night when the flight
of the yellow bird is unseen so no-one knows where
it's been till it opens its beak and speaks secrets ranging
beyond tears and grief to a comfort that's strange as
a bird on the wing for a man clamped in a square tin can,
sealed in a vacuum.

Sharks and Rainbows

Though you swim with dolphins,
you wear a hard hat
and nerves drill and hammer at your brow.

Though you lie on a tropical beach and smile,
you share an umbrella with despair;
you dance and sing like a dervish but

the swirl of movement is sand in your brain
blotting out all conviction;
and though you lean into hope

through rainbow dreams, black moods squat
on your shoulders like mud sacks
and keep you from bonding with trust.

Weeping Woman

*(Thoughts of Picasso and Dora Maar as they observe
his portrait of her*)*

He dislocates my face with sorrow,
        deconstructs my mouth, chills it blue,
plunders the black and white of me;
            needs me to weep, roar, fragment
                so he can dissect
        and butcher me like scrag end of mutton;

I paint her flaunting velvet hat, tilt it into madness,
slice the many-coloured pieces of clown-mask from her face
to show on canvas flesh scraped bare -

He displaces my eyes, crossing them with unshed tears,
twists the cheerful red and yellow of my hat,
then with loaded brush stabs a blaze of blue on its brim.
    He paints me in blood and acid (a footnote
        to the larger tableau of war), signs the canvas
with a flourish, a warrant for my slaughter

I fragment her bones, sections of white finger clutching
jags of grief; I dissect her screams in vomit-blue
            and splinter her teeth to sharpen the bite

*Picasso painted Weeping Woman in 1937, the same year he
finished Guernica)

Red Cross Man

white sash stained with blood,
stands beneath my window
collecting gossip – and silver.

Hunter

A slab of meat man,
hot in red tailored jacket,
smiles, primed for the kill.

In town he'll chase companies.
Here foxes will do. Same blood.

Season's End

Autumn-moon terrace,
dry leaves shuffle at night;
sprinklers cascade.

Summer's Over

round the pool chair
wasps thin
into autumn

Autumn

Drenched roses mould, sulk.
Days dwindle in rust-clear light.
Plum harvests its fruit.

Inbox @ 8.41

you send me your pain by e mail,
stark tale strung out in blood-red caps.

I'd just forgiven him, the old bastard
with his broken peg teeth and ginger hair.

Delete. A tiny crimson flag warns
of new credentials you present for him

glaring in lines of schoolgirl blue,
a naked shot of colour. Recoiling,

I shut down my screen. It flashes,
pales, blanks into silence

At Night

      fear
          stalks
              the
                  attic
                  fingers the newly oiled door
                     makes the bare boards groan
                  his square-shaped shadow
                  angled
             towards her
        while she
    starched awake
   in frost-white sheets
hardly dare
         dart
    a hand
      to clutch
             her   slippy
                   satin eiderdown
    knowing   then
    he would smell
her smallness

VII

Death by Statistics

Though officially dead,
(axed by insurers' predictions), you're different now
in the way you're alive, my love. You let me hack
and trim your wild, post-chemo hair; fly south
to dip in the Med by moonlight, make love at dawn,
create a new-man wardrobe
in a sluice of aquas, olives, ochres and sky-blues –
bright reflections of the *Côte d'Azur*.

With your friend,
who survived the same cancer,
you mirrored, compared cut-away stomachs, no-go foods,
minute weight-gains, ups-and-downs of spirit,
the curse of wind balloons bursting in the guts.
Walking in each other's moccasins, you measured
your footprints one against the other. But

now that he's dead,
something's changed. Though you still slump
round the house with your grumpy-old-man mug
and unbrushed teeth – a price on your head –
as I watch you baste in the sun, love,
you're pushing away statistics and I'm noticing
you've finally chosen to live.

Memory Boxes

i.m. Nessa

I remember you remembering me - how straight off,
with deep-dipping smile, you pinned me to my name
though yours had totally swum away from me.

Velvet boxes, made with your girls to hold memories of you,
afterwards are alive with your scent as they both
drop in snippets of this trip, that glance, this joke, that day,

a rag-bag of throw-away remarks, giggles, family legends -
while here, overwhelming this vast room, we celebrate you
by adding our own scribbled recollections. Memories

connect, collected on cards that curl into *whys?*;
cards that lie flattened in the boxes, crushed by sadness
or burst into colours, strong as maternal zest.

All I know of you – that luminous clarity of face – even
my leaky memory won't forget. Sensing your presence,
I remember what truly matters – not your name but you.

Sheila

Hunched over life,
bearing down on death,
your eyes were dimmed,
their birdlike twinkle done
– yet still your cheek was downy,
good to kiss.
Softness of fleeting sun
broke briefly
through the blanket mists
in which you huddled,
crabbed with sickness.
That slight curve of smile
wispily owned
just for a flash
old love in the shrivelled frame
before dark clouds once more
wrapped you in.
Even in your dying
you were soft of hue
like a water-bird,
and the gentle glow of your life
warmed and coloured mine.

Flight Path Unknown

Lost in attic dust,
a paper plane –
cockpit crumpled.

Moths

So easy to kill,
their wing-flit squashed,
dust on my fingers.

Gone

Life ends in a box
borne by men in working black.
We kiss your coldness.

You're gone, that's clear, but who's here
ruffled in cheap blue satin?

Ash

Beslan massacre, 2004

Ash has no name.
They're 'lucky' those who can mourn
bodies or bodies in body-bags.

On black-plastic mounds,
mothers slump, cling to photos,
choke on nameless ash

and plant shrines of water-flasks
from which their young, once thirsty,
will never drink.

Ground Zero

October 31st 2005

Caught between
All Souls
and All Saints,
here is a space
defined by rubble,
the lost waiting,
buildings scaffolded
or dead.

No pumpkins,
no tricks or spells –
but a bleak hiatus,
prayers hovering
round phantom towers
that lean sky-high
with the sway,
twins whispering
in the cross-winds
as they shudder.

Fear floats
down floor
after tumbled floor
to ashen sidewalks
where spectral relatives
squat, fenced by flowers
and photo flags
signed in the ink
of unfinished business

VIII

Charting the Tides

Sea thrashes the slump-backed Cobb that rounds
the surf at Lyme, wearing away – over centuries –
its hard stone strength. We try to regulate our beaches
with flags and notices; to predict, calculate, tabulate
the tides (high and low), times of sunrise and sunset;
print figures in booklets (Dorset pink, a pound a throw -
No liability for exceptional weather conditions).

Life tides, uncharted, swirl and trick us, some rising on a wave
of pills and pacemakers, washing over the old high-water mark
of three score year and ten – some falling, prematurely scuppered.

The beach, where tides gather and turn, has evolved
into a memorial garden, blackened by tar, encrusted
with metal junk from lost cargo and ships that have died;
two red flags, lifeless and torn by unfamiliar storms;
scraps of tiny sea creatures trapped in fossil spirals;
late features of cliff, crashed and ground to grit; shells
empty of life, broken and crunched into fragments;

We strengthen our sea walls with shingle, peg the hill with rods,
buy time – while waves falter, dissolving to a quieter rhythm,
foam absorbed into sand, footprints smoothed out by sea.

Rising Seas

at Lyme

Cliff-stubble
of   silver   spine-rods
will
pin   the   slide,
they say.

South –
on   crumbling   shores
masked   in
shingle   seaweed   wet sand   –
machines
dig   deep
lift,   scoop,

scrape
ancient   bones,
carve   new   contours,
face-lift
jutting   features –
a   front
against   breaking   tides.

Sea   and   hill
wait
while   a   million   pinpricks
wink
flirting
with   waste.

Hum of Bluebells

half-belled, half-budded, they electrify the wood,
plugged live into sunlight like a million mini-bulbs
coding and glowing in bells of pearled glass.

Each year I'm stunned by the lift and float, energy
of violet-blue vibrations radiant from shadow-clearing
blossom that hides winter-mould underfoot.

What force can throw the switch on spring
to power such a surge it makes essential colours hum,
the fragrance of the blue wood zing?

Word Rope

Climb
a rope −
do something different.

Play the line,
monkey with rhythm,
hang on its swing,
pendulum slow or
jerky, peevish.

Twist into simile,
bind sense tight,
cut out, cut down.
Feel the rope run,
new hands,

sand flowing
through open fingers.
Weigh, measure,
palm it into being,
knowing words may

fray, graze, burn
the soft-skinned
or else carry
the anchor's weight as it
drops through rings
of widening ripples
deep into
silence

Against the Flow

Scarf tangled in wind;
I run for a bus
that never comes.

Green Shawl

Stretching from sleep, hug
wool, soft-wrapped round cold waking.
Together we sit.

At Meditation

mind walks off;
here, now,
the bell rings.

Monkey-Mind*

Zen term for meditating with scattered mind

loops
          the loop of boredom,
tying up space with its antics;
            tail curls round the past,
       trying it for size
squeezing close,
          memories thrown to the wind,
titbits of distraction,
     while   quick fingers
        pick and scrabble
    at worries,
meticulous as bank clerks,
   who sort, count, bag up
       the small change of daily life.

              Plans bunch
     in a babble of head-talk,
        huddled like banana clusters,
     while mind shins up
the cage mesh,
    clutches at over-ripe fruit,
         spits out undigested seeds
    and blackened skins from old ideas;

        springs   across possible stillness
   to chatter and protest,
collecting fears like fleas,
         tempted towards an itch,
    which, once scratched, ceases,
having tricked the mind from concentration;

leaps   across an ice-lined ditch,
            swinging perilously
between opposite banks
          before it lands on a less familiar perch
        and there, counting breaths,
          waits for snow to fall –
   silent
              still
                     white.

Here and Now

At our letterbox,
    solid and woody,
the postman delivers
    word from other worlds,
his motorbike
    winding its stony way
down the bright lane,
    through leafless vineyards,
newly pruned,
    linking us up and down
to past and future.

Movement stops
    here and now
with the winter-warm sun.
    At midday
while the vines sleep, it's quiet,
    people don't rush;
the only activity
    an inner dance of creation
bubbling, shouting,
    insisting
it be heard in verse.

Cow-Time

The motorway has passed them by.
Standing four-square, deep in autumn meadow,
or cudding quietly round rough stone tracks,
they move in calm configurations, untidying
ochre fields, parted and combed by tractors.

In sudden temper, sky sluice-gates growl open,
work to a black and white shine the solitary Friesian.
The others – Herefords, Jerseys and Charollais –
gleam mahogany, chestnut, butter-cream,
solid as vintage motors lathered and richly rinsed.

With lenses blurred by fuggy breath and jets of rain
I sense their dark goggle-eyes tracking me,
hear pats plop and smack the ground between us.
Restless over my waterlogged plans, soaked otter-sleek,
I watch them watching me, wonder what they think.

This deluge will stop – or it will not. Either way,
undaunted, they stand and steam, grounded in grass.
Glasses off, beyond blind spots and misted vision,
there in the patient outline of their presence
I glimpse new patterns, a cow-time way of being.

Also by June Hall

The Now of Snow
published by Belgrave Press at £7.99

(title poem below)

The Now of Snow

An early snowplough's cleared the mountain road,
heaped crystals on either side,
banks that fall into deep-sleeping whiteness.

Puppy-children tumble out, pant heat into crisp air,
yelp and snowstorm one another, belly-flop in
sharp-edged drifts high and soft enough to bury them.

Whooping, they scoop powder-balls, brickbats
to launch against the car while we, caged in warmth,
gaze through a screen exploding with snow,

foresee hands, iced red, too numb to warm,
sodden trouser legs that cling to frozen skin,
feet stuck in shoes heavy with slush, the crying

and the long journey home. Worry shadows the sun.
Somewhere we've grown old.
We nag and fret over wet socks and the lack of boots.

What, for God's sake, is a wet sock
to the dazzle of the moment, the now of snow?

*Send orders to Melia Publishing Services, The White House,
2a Meadrow, Godalming, Surrey, GU3 7HN*